MW01093340

SACRAMENTAL ACTS
The Love Poems of Kenneth Rexroth

EDITED AND WITH AN INTRODUCTION BY
Sam Hamill *&* Elaine Laura Kleiner

COPPER CANYON PRESS

The publication of this book was supported by grants from the Lannan Founda-
tion, the National Endowment for the Arts, and the Washington State Arts Com-
mission, and by contributions from Elliott Bay Book Company, James Laughlin,
and the members of the Friends of Copper Canyon Press.

Library of Congress Cataloging-in-Publication Data

Rexroth, Kenneth, 1905–1982
Sacramental acts : the love poems of Kenneth Rexroth
p. cm.
"Except as noted, these poems were selected from One Hundred Poems from the
Japanese (1955); One Hundred Poems from the Chinese (1956); The Collected
Shorter Poems of Kenneth Rexroth (1966); Love and the Turning Year: One Hun-
dred More Poems from the Chinese (1970); The Orchid Boat: Women Poets of
China (1972); One Hundred More Poems from the Japanese (1974); Flower Wreath
Hill (1976); The Burning Heart: Women Poets of Japan (1977); Li Ch'ing-chao:
Complete Poems (1979)."
ISBN 1-55659-080-6 (pbk.)
1. Love poetry, American. I. Title.
PS3535.E923A6 1997
811.52–dc21   97-33928

COPPER CANYON PRESS

P.O. BOX 271, PORT TOWNSEND, WASHINGTON 98368

Acknowledgments

EXCEPT AS NOTED, these poems were selected from *One Hundred Poems from the Japanese* (1955); *One Hundred Poems from the Chinese* (1956); *The Collected Shorter Poems of Kenneth Rexroth* (1966); *Love and the Turning Year: One Hundred More Poems from the Chinese* (1970); *The Orchid Boat: Women Poets of China* (1972); *One Hundred More Poems from the Japanese* (1974); *Flower Wreath Hill* (1976); *The Burning Heart: Women Poets of Japan* (1977); *Li Ch'ing-chao: Complete Poems* (1979), all published by New Directions and reprinted here thanks to special arrangements made through the generosity of James Laughlin, Publisher, and his staff.

The translations of the two poems by Asklepiades were originally published in *Poems from the Greek Anthology* (The University of Michigan Press, 1962). The translation of Raphael Alberti's "Homecoming of Love on the Summits of the Wind" originally appeared in *Thirty Spanish Poems of Love and Exile* (City Lights Pocket Poets #2, 1956).

Special thanks are also due to Bradford Morrow, Rexroth's literary executor, for his cooperation and assistance, as to Rexroth's widow, Carol Tinker.

CONTENTS

II TRANSLATIONS

III

INTRODUCTION

BY TURNS revolutionary and conservative, simultaneously spiritual and worldly, Asian and Western, Kenneth Rexroth created what must surely be regarded as the most original synthesis of transcendent metaphysical and erotic verse ever written by an American poet. A polyglot iconoclast, Rexroth was steeped in the world's spiritual and literary traditions, absorbing ideas and philosophy into his poetry and prose all his life. The author of nearly sixty books, including translations of poetry from Chinese, Japanese, Greek, Latin, Italian, French, Spanish, Swedish, and other languages, and two volumes of *Classics Revisited* among several volumes of essays, he was one of the most original and universal literary scholars of this century. William Carlos Williams, reviewing the philosophical *The Phoenix and the Tortoise* (1944), remarked, "Let me say that this is one of the most completely realized arguments I have encountered in a book of verse in my time."

But nowhere is Rexroth's verse more fully realized than in his erotic poetry. While he continuously celebrated matrimonial relationships, he also refused to pretend that he did not enjoy daydreams of "copulating with sixteen year old nymphomaniacs of my imagination" in a poem probably inspired by a Catullan precedent. No doubt he made use of that ugly, sterile-sounding Latinate verb precisely because such imaginings are without love. In contrast, his love poems, like priestly offerings, raise all that is beautiful in this world so that it may be seen freshly transformed into the body of the sacred. In his famous "A Letter to William Carlos Williams," another kind of love poem, Rexroth defines the role of the poet as "one who creates sacramental relationships that last always." In his poetry the profane becomes the sacrament, the diurnal, mundane moment suddenly made luminous by perceptions that positively resonate with philosophical and historical content. Within the parameters of such a deep spirituality, he could remain astonishingly profane at times. He delighted in telling audiences, "I write poetry to seduce women and to overthrow the capitalist system. In *that* order." And yet the poetry transcends mere human sexuality, eroticism becoming but an emblem of the synthesis of self and other, the sacred revealed within the profane world, the light of eternal love exposed in temporal flesh.

Born December 22, 1905, in South Bend, Indiana, to a German-American family impoverished by his father's alcoholism and his mother's poor health, Rexroth was schooled at home and by age four was reading history, arithmetic, astronomy, and natural science under the tutelage of his mother, Delia. He continued until his mother's death in 1916 and the death of his father in 1918, when he moved to Chicago to live with an aunt and enrolled in the Chicago Art Institute at age thirteen. During his years in Chicago, his self-education continued, often aided by the company of musicians, artists, anarchists, Wobblies, communists, and gangsters.

Several years later he moved to Greenwich Village with a paramour and joined the New School for Social Research before dropping out to serve a stint as a postulant in a New York monastery. At nineteen, he hitchhiked across the country, working as wrangler, fire watch, soda jerk, and at other odd jobs until, in Hoboken, he signed on as mess steward on a steamer traveling to Mexico, Buenos Aires, and eventually to Paris, where he met, among others, Tristan Tzara and the surrealists.

He married a commercial artist from Chicago, Andrée Schafer, in 1927, and the impoverished young couple hitchhiked to Seattle for their honeymoon, then on down the West Coast to San Francisco where he worked as a maritime union organizer and established himself in the intellectual and political community. He would remain in San Francisco for forty years.

In 1940, while Rexroth was working on behalf of Japanese-Americans who faced, he believed, immanent dangers, and was frustrated at making little headway, his first volume of poetry, *In What Hour*, was published by Macmillan. It received a number of reviews that were at best naive and at worst nasty and condescending. Rolphe Humphries called Rexroth "a simple-minded man with a liking for outdoors." Horace Gregory dismissed his work as mere "regional verse that reflected the charms of the Pacific Coast." (Writing in 1984 with a little historical perspective, Robert Hass credited *In What Hour* with "inventing the culture of the West Coast.") To complicate matters, his marriage was falling apart and he was called to register with the local draft board despite being almost thirty-five. Eventually, he registered as a conscientious objector.

In October, 1940, Andrée Rexroth, the poet's wife of thirteen years, lost her lifelong struggle with an inherited brain disease with symptoms similar to epilepsy. The poet was crushed. He had met Marie Kass earlier at a nurses' union meeting and he married her within the year. Rexroth spent the war years serving as an attendant in a psychiatric ward in San Francisco, and the Rexroth apartment became the center for a weekly literary discussion group and a meeting place for anarchists and antiwar protesters, as well as a secret convalescent center for Japanese-Americans seeking an escape from internment camps. The poems he would write for Andrée would immortalize his sense of love lost without reference to the collapse of their relationship at the end of her life. No doubt the broken marriage intensified his sense of loss as he remembered moments of sublime harmony with her. The primary influence behind these elegies is Yuan Chen, T'ang Dynasty poet and friend of Po Chu-i revered especially for several elegies following the death of his wife. Rexroth had gone to school on Arthur Waley's and other translations of Asian classics in the thirties, after Witter Bynner had introduced him to the great Tu Fu in the twenties. It was also during the war years that he began translating *The Greek Anthology*, working first from a bilingual edition to refresh the little ancient Greek he had learned as a child.

His marriage to Marie ended in 1948, and Rexroth threw himself into his work on Pacifica Radio and at the Poetry Center he'd helped found (with Ruth Witt-Diamant) at San Francisco State University. He was a regular contributor to *The Nation*, the *San Francisco Chronicle*, *Saturday Review*, and other journals, including the *New York Times*.

In 1949, during a trip to Europe, Rexroth was joined by Marthe Larsen, whom he married in Aix-en-Provence despite still being married to Marie. They returned, Marthe pregnant, in December, and in five years the couple had two daughters, Mary and Katherine. Marthe and their daughters inspired some of the most remarkable love poetry in our language. Marie remained close to the family, a lifelong friend and godmother to both daughters. Her divorce from the poet was not filed until 1955.

By the mid-fifties, Rexroth had become the most prominent figure in what would later be known as the San Francisco Renaissance, presiding over the most famous poetry reading of this century, a reading proposed by a painter, Wally Hedrick, to be held at the Six Gallery, a tiny former auto-repair shop on Fillmore Street. Rexroth was master of ceremonies the night of October 13, 1955,

introducing the poets Gary Snyder, Philip Whalen, Michael Mc-
Clure, Philip Lamantia, and Allen Ginsberg. The small audience
included a noisy, excited Jack Kerouac, Neal Cassady, Gregory
Corso, and Lawrence Ferlinghetti. Rexroth, dressed in a second-
hand suit, stepped up to a grape crate in front of the audience and
declared, "This is a lectern for a midget who is going to recite the
Iliad in haiku form." Ginsberg recited his new poem, "Howl," while
Kerouac beat out rhythms on a winejug. Three years later, Kerouac
would immortalize the evening in his *The Dharma Bums*.

Rexroth's fallout with the Beat Generation came one evening
not long after the Six Gallery reading when a rude, drunken Ker-
ouac arrived hours late for a dinner at Rexroth's home, and with
Ginsberg, Snyder, and Whalen in tow, demanded more booze.
Rexroth pitched a fit. Ginsberg announced his superiority over
Rexroth as a poet, and the evening came to an abrupt halt with the
departing Kerouac yelling, "Dirty German!" over and over outside
and at the top of his lungs. Several years later, *Time* magazine, in
an article on the San Francisco Renaissance, would call Rexroth
"father of the Beats," to which he replied, "An entomologist is not
a bug!"

By 1956, Marthe was worn out with her endless chores – serving
as primary source of household income, secretary, co-translator,
correspondent, chief servant and supply sergeant for a demanding
poet. She met and fell in love with the poet Robert Creeley, and
made no effort to conceal her feelings. Rexroth fell into fits of de-
pression, rage, and paranoia. He accused Ginsberg (wrongly) of
promoting Creeley's affair with Marthe, and fretted over imaginary
plots. He wrote of this time in "Marthe Away," later published as
"She Is Away,"

For one heartbeat the
Heart was free and moved itself. O love,
I who am lost and damned with words,
Whose words are a business and an art,
I have no words. These words, this poem, this
Is all confusion and ignorance.

When Marthe left, he begged her to return, promising to under-
take therapy and make substantial changes in the way they lived.
But it was too late. Marie and Rexroth's dear friend James Laughlin,
publisher of New Directions, assuaged him as best they could
while the furies overcame him. In October of 1956, *Poetry* maga-
zine published his "Seven Poems for Marthe, My Wife." Rexroth's
condition deteriorated so much that Marthe returned, fearing he
might be suicidal. Marie and Laughlin again provided some much-
needed financial aid.

Misdirected rages brought an end to several of Rexroth's friend-
ships during those years. The only periods of calm seem to have
come while he was writing or when he was with his daughters,
or in the company of his few intimate friends. In the poems he
achieved a calmness of heart and mind, a sense of grace his daily
life did not contain. He campaigned tirelessly on behalf of the
poetry of Denise Levertov, Snyder, Whalen, Lamantia and others,
despite his often stormy relationships with the poets themselves.

During a month-long journey to New York, Rexroth received a
letter from Marthe begging him not to return. He had received a
$1,000 Shelley Prize from the Poetry Society of America, and he
was writing for *Esquire* and other journals, leading Marthe to be-
lieve that perhaps an amicable separation could be made. It was
not to be. The following year the family set off for Aix-en-Provence

on an Amy Lowell Poetry Fellowship, visiting Italy in 1959. But his literary successes did nothing to ease tensions in the family, and in 1961, Marthe left and filed for divorce. Rexroth learned to live alone, but his wild emotional ride continued as he alternately disparaged Marthe and wrote her impassioned love letters. When New Directions planned to publish his "new and selected poems," *Natural Numbers*, in 1963, he removed Marthe's name from the poems he had written for her.

Carol Tinker became Rexroth's partner and assistant, much happier in such a role than Marthe had ever been, and the poet enjoyed growing popularity. Several small awards made it possible for Rexroth, Carol, and his daughter Mary to travel around much of the world in 1967, ending their journey with a visit to Gary Snyder who was then living in Kyoto.

Offered a year-to-year teaching job at the University of California in Santa Barbara beginning in 1968, Rexroth, wanting a little financial security for the first time in his life, accepted, and with Carol Tinker left San Francisco. In a notebook he kept during the first days in Santa Barbara, he noted, "I lived forty years in San Francisco and haven't a real friend to show for it." And yet he had performed with some of the best jazz musicians in the world and written with greater and broader knowledge and with more diversity than any poet of his generation. He had been a major contributor to leading literary journals and brought poetry to the airwaves.

He bought a house in Montecito and had his huge library shipped down the coast. He was enormously popular with students, especially when he disparaged "the fog factory" of the English Department, and announced that too many university students at "Surfboard Tech" were "either stoned or illiterate or both." His outbursts were funny and enlightening, but they also made enemies. The university "pink-slipped" him in 1973, saying he was too old to teach any longer.

He settled into his relationship with Carol Tinker. Theirs was more a partnership of souls than a conventional husband-and-wife relationship, but when he received a Fulbright Fellowship to visit Japan in 1974, he thought it best that they be legally married, and so they were.

His last years were his happiest. Despite his falling out with Ginsberg, Snyder, Duncan, and others, he continued to champion their poetry. In many ways, he had become "feminized" through translating the great Sung Dynasty poet Li Ch'ing-chao (working with the scholar Ling Chung) and an anthology of Chinese women poets, *The Orchid Boat*. He invented Marichiko, writing a volume of poems in the voice of "a young Japanese woman poet," and translated classical and modern Japanese women poets. His biographer, Linda Hamalian, suggests, "Translating the work of women poets from China and Japan reveals a transformation of both heart and mind."

Another Rexroth scholar, Morgan Gibson, has written extensively in two books about the deepening influence of Shingon Buddhism late in the poet's life. In *Revolutionary Rexroth* (Archon Books, 1986), he writes of Rexroth's conviction that "poetry originates in personal vision (communion with others) [sic], takes form in the direct communication of living speech, person-to-person, and functions sacramentally in community." Rexroth himself had said that his spiritual aim "was to move from abandon, to erotic mysticism, from erotic mysticism to the ethical mysticism of sacramental marriage, thence to the realization of the ethical mysticism of universal responsibility." If his domestic life was often troubled, no doubt a significant part of that difficulty was the result of the poet's attraction to strong, independent-minded women.

In any case, he enjoyed his life, playing the aging *enfant terrible* at poetry readings, performing with *koto* and *shakuhachi* accompaniment. Although he was sometimes indefensibly difficult and often turbulent, he exhibited all his life a profound devotion to the way of poetry, and was equally capable of almost boundless generosity. His love poems realize a sense of completion, an abiding sense of unity. If they are idealized in comparison to his daily life, it makes no difference. The poetry remains.

In December, 1980, Rexroth suffered a heart attack and was bedridden for several months, during which time he worked on a festschrift honoring James Laughlin, observing, "I wouldn't have had a career without Laughlin, and I look on [him] as my best friend." The following spring, Rexroth suffered a stroke, forcing his wife to rush him to Cottage Hospital in Santa Barbara. Late that summer, he suffered a second (and much more severe) stroke, that left him virtually unable to speak. He required round-the-clock nursing that Medicare and Blue Cross would not cover, and in September, his "best friend" Laughlin stepped in once again, providing funds for Rexroth to be cared for at home. The last six months of his life were plagued by a worn-out body giving in to the ravages of time – congestive heart failure, an inoperative hernia, kidney failure, yet another stroke, and even periods of paralysis. But he was fond of his young nurse and during times when his memory for words functioned, he would scrawl "Call Carol," or "I'm hungry," on his small blackboard.

He died June 6, 1982, of a massive heart attack that blew out the fuse of the electrocardiogram machine that was monitoring him.

He was buried in Santa Barbara in a simple grave on a hill over-
looking the Pacific Ocean. His epitaph is a poem from *The Silver
Swan* (Copper Canyon Press, 1976):

> As the full moon rises
> The swan sings
> In sleep
> On the lake of the mind

It is remarkable that a life as deeply troubled as that of Kenneth
Rexroth should produce erotic poetry of such profound transcen-
dence. It is remarkable, but not that extraordinary considering
how often real genius is accompanied by personal suffering and/or
insufferable behavior. Whether writing of idealized love, of love
lost, of a father's boundless love, or of the deepest spiritual engage-
ment, he achieved again and again in his poetry exactly what he
most longed for but could not find in his life: a passionate but
utterly calm self-transcendent state of infinite connectedness. In
the love poems, even the longing resonates with classical over-
tones, the poet's staggering erudition informing poems so trans-
lucent, so transparent as to be confused with simple-mindedness
by a Eurocentric critic.

In poetry, Kenneth Rexroth, orphan polyglot iconoclast and
autodidact, great man of letters with virtually total recall, agit-
propagandist and anti-establishment activist, ecologist and
scholar, could finally transform desire into something larger than
either or both of the lovers themselves. He achieved something
almost impossibly simple – a glimpse of sacramental grace within
our temporal flesh in a fragile, perishing world. "Erotic love," he
was fond of saying, "is one of the highest forms of contemplation."

Written from the haunted and celebrated depths of a life lived to the fullest, Rexroth's love poetry transcends his personal suffering, realizing an ascendant universalization of experience.

It is sad to note that Kenneth Rexroth sometimes bit the very hands that might have fed him, but his commitment to truth and a revolutionary lifestyle far out-weighed his concerns for self-promotion. His anti-establishmentarianism cost him dearly: his work is almost never included in major anthologies, and yet the nature of so much of the work itself bears the undeniable and indelible handprint of genius – not only in the poetry, but also in his essays. In his recent study of Rexroth's shorter poetry, *The Holiness of the Real* (Fairleigh Dickinson University Press, 1996), Donald Gutierrez points out that Rexroth was stigmatized by advocating on behalf of the Beats and poets like Robert Duncan, and that Rexroth has been further victimized by being found "politically incorrect" (once again) by the present status quo. That he spent a lifetime encouraging literacy in general and poetry in particular and that he was uniquely generous to so many poets, both elder and younger, is beyond dispute. He did more to encourage publication of writing by young women than any other prominent white male of the sixties or seventies, and he established a scholarship for young women writers in Japan. And equally beyond dispute are the fact and beauty of so much of his work. It remains to be explored, like a great snowcapped peak rising at the edge of the Pacific.

SAM HAMILL   ELAINE LAURA KLEINER
PORT TOWNSEND   TERRE HAUTE

SACRAMENTAL ACTS

I

A DIALOGUE OF WATCHING

Let me celebrate you. I
Have never known anyone
More beautiful than you. I
Walking beside you, watching
You move beside me, watching
That still grace of hand and thigh,
Watching your face change with words
You do not say, watching your
Solemn eyes as they turn to me,
Or turn inward, full of knowing,
Slow or quick, watching your full
Lips part and smile or turn grave,
Watching your narrow waist, your
Proud buttocks in their grace, like
A sailing swan, an animal,
Free, your own, and never
To be subjugated, but
Abandoned, as I am to you,
Overhearing your perfect
Speech of motion, of love and
Trust and security as
You feed or play with our children.
I have never known any
One more beautiful than you.

BETWEEN MYSELF AND DEATH

to Jimmy Blanton's Music:
SOPHISTICATED LADY, BODY AND SOUL

A fervor parches you sometimes,
And you hunch over it, silent,
Cruel, and timid; and sometimes
You are frightened with wantonness,
And give me your desperation.
Mostly we lurk in our coverts,
Protecting our spleens, pretending
That our bandages are our wounds.
But sometimes the wheel of change stops;
Illusion vanishes in peace;
And suddenly pride lights your flesh –
Lucid as diamond, wise as pearl –
And your face, remote, absolute,
Perfect and final like a beast's.
It is wonderful to watch you,
A living woman in a room
Full of frantic, sterile people,
And think of your arching buttocks
Under your velvet evening dress,
And the beautiful fire spreading
From your sex, burning flesh and bone,
The unbelievably complex
Tissues of your brain all alive
Under your coiling, splendid hair.

*

I like to think of you naked.
I put your naked body
Between myself alone and death.
If I go into my brain
And set fire to your sweet nipples,
To the tendons beneath your knees,
I can see far before me.
It is empty there where I look,
But at least it is lighted.

I know how your shoulders glisten,
How your face sinks into trance,
And your eyes like a sleepwalker's,
And your lips of a woman
Cruel to herself.
                    I like to
Think of you clothed, your body
Shut to the world and self-contained,
Its wonderful arrogance
That makes all women envy you.
I can remember every dress,
Each more proud then a naked nun.
When I go to sleep my eyes
Close in a mesh of memory.
Its cloud of intimate odor
Dreams instead of myself.

You open your
Dress on the dusty
Bed where no one
Has slept for years
An owl moans on the roof
You say
My dear my
Dear
In the smoky light of the old
Oil lamp your shoulders
Belly breasts buttocks
Are all like peach blossoms
Huge stars far away far apart
Outside the cracked window pane
Immense immortal animals
Each one only an eye
Watch
You open your body
No end to the night
No end to the forest
House abandoned for a lifetime
In the forest in the night
No one will ever come
To the house
Alone
In the black world
In the country of eyes

OAXACA 1925

You were a beautiful child
With troubled face, green eyelids
And black lace stockings
We met in a filthy bar
You said
"My name is Nada
I don't want anything from you
I will not take from you
I will give you nothing"
I took you home down alleys
Splattered with moonlight and garbage and cats
To your desolate disheveled room
Your feet were dirty
The lacquer was chipped on your fingernails
We spent a week hand in hand
Wandering entranced together
Through a sweltering summer
Of guitars and gunfire and tropical leaves
And black shadows in the moonlight
A lifetime ago

GRADUALISM

We slept naked
On top of the covers and woke
In the chilly dawn and crept
Between the warm sheets and made love
In the morning you said
"It snowed last night on the mountain"
High up on the blue-black diorite
Faint orange streaks of snow
In the ruddy dawn
I said
"It has been snowing for months
All over Canada and Alaska
And Minnesota and Michigan
Right now wet snow is falling
In the morning streets of Chicago
Bit by bit they are making over the world
Even in Mexico even for us"

Nests in the eaves stir in the dawn
Ephemeral as our peace
Morning prayer
Grace before food
I understand
The endless sky the small earth
The shadow cone
Your shining
Lips and eyes
Your thighs drenched with the sea
A telescope full of fireflies
Innumerable nebulae all departing
Ten billion years before we ever met

All night I lay awake beside you,
Leaning on my elbow, watching your
Sleeping face, that face whose purity
Never ceases to astonish me.
I could not sleep. But I did not want
Sleep nor miss it. Against my body,
Your body lay like a warm soft star.
How many nights I have waked and watched
You, in how many places. Who knows?
This night might be the last one of all.
As on so many nights, once more I
Drank from your sleeping flesh the deep still
Communion I am not always strong
Enough to take from you waking, the peace of love.
Foggy lights moved over the ceiling
Of our room, so like the rooms of France
And Italy, rooms of honeymoon,
And gave your face an ever-changing
Speech, the secret communication
Of untellable love. I knew then,
As your secret spoke, my secret self,
The blind bird, hardly visible in
An endless web of lies. And I knew
The web too, its every knot and strand,
The hidden crippled bird, the terrible web.
Towards the end of night, as trucks rumbled
In the streets, you stirred, cuddled to me,
And spoke my name. Your voice was the voice
Of a girl who had never known loss

Of love, betrayal, mistrust, or lie.
And later you turned again and clutched
My hand and pressed it to your body.
Now I know surely and forever,
However much I have blotted our
Waking love, its memory is still
There. And I know the web, the net,
The blind and crippled bird. For then, for
One brief instant it was not blind, nor
Trapped, nor crippled. For one heartbeat the
Heart was free and moved itself. O love,
I who am lost and damned with words,
Whose words are a business and an art,
I have no words. These words, this poem, this
Is all confusion and ignorance.
But I know that coached by your sweet heart,
My heart beat one free beat and sent
Through all my flesh the blood of truth.

MOCKING BIRDS

In mid-March in the heart of
The night, in the center of
The sterile city, in the
Midst of miles of asphalt and
Stone, alone and frustrated,
Wakeful on my narrow bed,
My brain spinning with worry,
There came to me, slipping through
The interstices of the
Blowing darkness, the living,
Almost imperceptible,
Faint, persistent, recurrent
Song of a single tree toad –
A voice sweeter than most birds.
Seven years ago we lay
Naked and moist, making love
Under the Easter full moon,
The thick fragrant light shaking
With the songs of mocking birds.

LONELINESS

To think of you surcharged with
Loneliness. To hear your voice
Over the recorder say,
"Loneliness." The word, the voice,
So full of it, and I, with
You away, so lost in it –
Lost in loneliness and pain.
Black and unendurable,
Thinking of you with every
Corpuscle of my flesh, in
Every instant of night
And day. O, my love, the times
We have forgotten love, and
Sat lonely beside each other.
We have eaten together,
Lonely behind our plates, we
Have hidden behind children,
We have slept together in
A lonely bed. Now my heart
Turns towards you, awake at last,
Penitent, lost in the last
Loneliness. Speak to me. Talk
To me. Break the black silence.
Speak of a tree full of leaves,
Of a flying bird, the new
Moon in the sunset, a poem,
A book, a person – all the
Casual healing speech
Of your resonant, quiet voice.
The word freedom. The word peace.

from THE THIN EDGE OF YOUR PRIDE

X

Out of the westborne snow shall come a memory
Floated upon it by my hands,
By my lips that remember your kisses.
It shall caress your hands, your lips,
Your breasts, your thighs, with kisses,
As real as flesh, as real as memory of flesh.
I shall come to you with the spring,
Spring's flesh in the world,
Translucent narcissus, dogwood like a vision,
And phallic crocus,
Spring's flesh in my hands.

CINQUE TERRE

A voice sobs on colored sand
Where colored horses run
Athwart the surf
Us alone in the universe
Where griefs move like the sea
Of the love lost
Under the morning star
Creeping down the sky
Into pale blind water
And we make love
At the very edge of the cliff
Where the vineyards end
In a fringe of ancient
Silver olive trees

CAMARGUE

Green moon blaze
Over violet dancers
Shadow heads catch fire
Forget forget
Forget awake aware dropping in the well
Where the nightingale sings
In the blooming pomegranate
You beside me
Like a colt swimming slowly in kelp
In the nude sea
Where ten thousand birds
Move like a waved scarf
On the long surge of sleep

AMONG THE CYPRESSES AT THE END
OF THE WAY OF THE CROSS

Will you eat watermelon
Or drink lemonade
Beside San Miniato
This hot twilight
Arno blurring in its white dry cobbled bed
Wine honey olive oil
Fill the air with their secret vapors
And a black potter
Treads treads treads
Her wheel shaping a pot
With a template cut from your flesh
Lovers whimper in the dusk
We are lost do you hear
We are all lost
As the hundred bells break
And the stars speak

THE WHEEL REVOLVES

You were a girl of satin and gauze
Now you are my mountain and waterfall companion.
Long ago I read those lines of Po Chu-i
Written in his middle age.
Young as I was they touched me.
I never thought in my own middle age
I would have a beautiful young dancer
To wander with me by falling crystal waters,
Among mountains of snow and granite,
Least of all that unlike Po's girl
She would be my very daughter.

The earth turns towards the sun.
Summer comes to the mountains.
Blue grouse drum in the red fir woods
All the bright long days.
You put blue jay and flicker feathers
In your hair.
Two and two violet green swallows
Play over the lake.
The blue birds have come back
To nest on the little island.
The swallows sip water on the wing
And play at love and dodge and swoop
Just like the swallows that swirl
Under and over the Ponte Vecchio.
Light rain crosses the lake
Hissing faintly. After the rain
There are giant puffballs with tortoise shell backs

At the edge of the meadow.
Snows of a thousand winters
Melt in the sun of one summer.
Wild cyclamen bloom by the stream.
Trout veer in the transparent current.
In the evening marmots bark in the rocks.
The Scorpion curls over the glimmering ice field.

A white-crowned night sparrow sings as the moon sets.
Thunder growls far off.
Our campfire is a single light
Amongst a hundred peaks and waterfalls.
The manifold voices of falling water
Talk all night.
Wrapped in your down bag
Starlight on your cheeks and eyelids
Your breath comes and goes
In a tiny cloud in the frosty night.
Ten thousand birds sing in the sunrise.
Ten thousand years revolve without change.
All this will never be again.

It is deep twilight, my wife
And girls are fixing supper
In the kitchen. I turn out
The reading lamp and rest my eyes.
Outside the window the snow
Has turned deep blue. *Antony*
and Cleopatra after a trying day. I think of
Those vigorous rachitic
Men and women taking off
Their clothes of lace and velvet
And gold brocade and climbing
Naked into bed together
Lice in their stinking perfumed
Armpits, the bed full of bugs.

A FLUTE OVERHEARD

Grey summer
Low tide the sea in the air
A flute song
In a neighboring house
Forty years ago
Socrates on death
The pages turn
The clear voice
Sea fog in the cypress
My daughter calls
From the next room
After forty years
A girl's candid face
Above my desk
Twenty-five years dead
Grey summer fog
And the smell of the living sea
A voice on the moving air
Reading Socrates on death

ON WHAT PLANET

Uniformly over the whole countryside
The warm air flows imperceptibly seaward;
The autumn haze drifts in deep bands
Over the pale water;
White egrets stand in the blue marshes;
Tamalpais, Diablo, St. Helena
Float in the air.
Climbing on the cliffs of Hunter's Hill
We look out over fifty miles of sinuous
Interpenetration of mountains and sea.

Leading up a twisted chimney,
Just as my eyes rise to the level
Of a small cave, two white owls
Fly out, silent, close to my face.
They hover, confused in the sunlight,
And disappear into the recesses of the cliff.

All day I have been watching a new climber,
A young girl with ash blond hair
And gentle confident eyes.
She climbs slowly, precisely,
With unwasted grace.
While I am coiling the ropes,
Watching the spectacular sunset,
She turns to me and says, quietly,
"It must be very beautiful, the sunset,
On Saturn, with the rings and all the moons."

WHEN WE WITH SAPPHO

"…about the cool water
the wind sounds through sprays
of apple, and from the quivering leaves
slumber pours down…"

We lie here in the bee filled, ruinous
Orchard of a decayed New England farm,
Summer in our hair, and the smell
Of summer in our twined bodies,
Summer in our mouths, and summer
In the luminous, fragmentary words
Of this dead Greek woman.
Stop reading. Lean back. Give me your mouth.
Your grace is as beautiful as a sleep.
You move against me like a wave
That moves in sleep.
Your body spreads across my brain
Like a bird-filled summer;
Not like a body, not like a separate thing,
But like a nimbus that hovers
Over every other thing in all the world.
Lean back. You are beautiful,
As beautiful as the folding
Of your hands in sleep.

We have grown old in the afternoon.
Here in our orchard we are as old
As she is now, wherever dissipate
In that distant sea her gleaming dust

Flashes in the wave crest
Or stains the murex shell.
All about us the old farm subsides
Into the honey-bearing chaos of high summer.
In those far islands the temples
Have fallen away, and the marble
Is the color of wild honey.
There is nothing left of the gardens
That were once about them, of the fat
Turf marked with cloven hooves.
Only the sea grass struggles
Over the crumbled stone,
Over the splintered steps,
Only the blue and yellow
Of the sea, and the cliffs
Red in the distance across the bay.
Lean back.
Her memory has passed to our lips now.
Our kisses fall through summer's chaos
In our own breasts and thighs.

Gold colossal domes of cumulus cloud
Lift over the undulant, sibilant forest.
The air presses against the earth.
Thunder breaks over the mountains.
Far off, over the Adirondacks,
Lightning quivers, almost invisible
In the bright sky, violet against
The grey, deep shadows of the bellied clouds.
The sweet virile hair of thunderstorms
Brushes over the swelling horizon.
Take off your shoes and stockings.

I will kiss your sweet legs and feet
As they lie half buried in the tangle
Of rank-scented midsummer flowers.
Take off your clothes. I will press
Your summer honeyed flesh into the hot
Soil, into the crushed, acrid herbage
Of midsummer. Let your body sink
Like honey through the hot
Granular fingers of summer.

Rest. Wait. We have enough for a while.
Kiss me with your mouth
Wet and ragged, your mouth that tastes
Of my own flesh. Read to me again
The twisting music of that language
That is of all others, itself a work of art.
Read again those isolate, poignant words
Saved by ancient grammarians
To illustrate the conjugations
And declensions of the more ancient dead.
Lean back in the curve of my body,
Press your bruised shoulders against
The damp hair of my body.
Kiss me again. Think, sweet linguist,
In this world the ablative is impossible.
No other one will help us here.
We must help ourselves to each other.
The wind walks slowly away from the storm;
Veers on the wooded crests; sounds
In the valleys. Here we are isolate,
One with the other; and beyond
This orchard lies isolation,

The isolation of all the world.
Never let anything intrude
On the isolation of this day,
These words, isolate on dead tongues,
This orchard, hidden from fact and history,
These shadows, blended in the summer light,
Together isolate beyond the world's reciprocity.

Do not talk any more. Do not speak.
Do not break silence until
We are weary of each other.
Let our fingers run like steel
Carving the contours of our bodies' gold.
Do not speak. My face sinks
In the clotted summer of your hair.
The sound of the bees stops.
Stillness falls like a cloud.
Be still. Let your body fall away
Into the awe-filled silence
Of the fulfilled summer –
Back, back, infinitely away –
Our lips weak, faint with stillness.

See. The sun has fallen away.
Now there are amber
Long lights on the shattered
Boles of the ancient apple trees.
Our bodies move to each other
As bodies move in sleep;
At once filled and exhausted,
As the summer moves to autumn,
As we, with Sappho, move toward death.

My eyelids sink toward sleep in the hot
Autumn of your uncoiled hair.
Your body moves in my arms
On the verge of sleep;
And it is as though I held
In my arms the bird filled
Evening sky of summer.

RUNAWAY

There are sparkles of rain on the bright
Hair over your forehead;
Your eyes are wet and your lips
Wet and cold, your cheek rigid with cold.
Why have you stayed
Away so long, why have you only
Come to me late at night
After walking for hours in wind and rain?
Take off your dress and stockings;
Sit in the deep chair before the fire.
I will warm your feet in my hands;
I will warm your breasts and thighs with kisses.
I wish I could build a fire
In you that would never go out.
I wish I could be sure that deep in you
Was a magnet to draw you always home.

INVERSELY, AS THE SQUARE OF
THEIR DISTANCES APART

It is impossible to see anything
In this dark; but I know this is me, Rexroth,
Plunging through the night on a chilling planet.
It is warm and busy in this vegetable
Darkness where invisible deer feed quietly.
The sky is warm and heavy, even the trees
Over my head cannot be distinguished,
But I know they are knobcone pines, that their cones
Endure unopened on the branches, at last
To grow imbedded in the wood, waiting for fire
To open them and reseed the burned forest.
And I am waiting, alone, in the mountains,
In the forest, in the darkness, and the world
Falls swiftly on its measured ellipse.

                    *

It is warm tonight and very still.
The stars are hazy and the river –
Vague and monstrous under the fireflies –
Is hardly audible, resonant
And profound at the edge of hearing.
I can just see your eyes and wet lips.
Invisible, solemn, and fragrant,
Your flesh opens to me in secret.
We shall know no further enigma.
After all the years there is nothing
Stranger than this. We who know ourselves

As one doubled thing, and move our limbs
As deft implements of one fused lust,
Are mysteries in each other's arms.

*

At the wood's edge in the moonlight
We dropped our clothes and stood naked,
Swaying, shadow mottled, enclosed
In each other and together
Closed in the night. We did not hear
The whippoorwill, nor the aspen's
Whisper; the owl flew silently
Or cried out loud, we did not know.
We could not hear beyond the heart.
We could not see the moving dark
And light, the stars that stood or moved,
The stars that fell. Did they all fall
We had not known. We were falling
Like meteors, dark through black cold
Toward each other, and then compact,
Blazing through air into the earth.

*

I lie alone in an alien
Bed in a strange house and morning
More cruel than any midnight
Pours its brightness through the window –
Cherry branches with the flowers
Fading, and behind them the gold
Stately baubles of the maple,

And behind them the pure immense
April sky and a white frayed cloud,
And in and behind everything,
The inescapable vacant
Distance of loneliness.

DELIA REXROTH

died June, 1916

Under your illkempt yellow roses,
Delia, today you are younger
Than your son. Two-and-a-half decades –
The family monument sagged askew,
And he overtook your half-a-life.
On the other side of the country,
Near the willows by the slow river,
Deep in the earth, the white ribs retain
The curve of your fervent, careful breast;
The fine skull, the ardor of your brain.
And in the fingers the memory
Of Chopin études, and in the feet
Slow waltzes and champagne twosteps sleep.
And the white full moon of midsummer,
That you watched awake all that last night,
Watches history fill the deserts
And oceans with corpses once again;
And looks in the east window at me,
As I move past you to middle age
And knowledge past your agony and waste.

STILL ON WATER

Solitude closes down around us
As we lie passive and exhausted
Solitude clamps us softly in its warm hand.
A turtle slips into the water
With a faint noise like a breaking bubble;
There is no other sound, only the dim
Momentous conversation of windless
Poplar and sycamore leaves and rarely,
A single, questioning frog voice.
I turn my eyes from your entranced face
And watch the oncoming sunset
Powder the immense, unblemished zenith
With almost imperceptible sparkles of gold.
Your eyes open, your head turns.
Your lips nibble at my shoulder.
I feel a languid shudder run over your body.
Suddenly you laugh, like a pure
Exulting flute, spring to your feet
And plunge into the water.
A white bird breaks from the rushes
And flies away, and the boat rocks
Drunkenly in the billows
Of your nude jubilation.

INCARNATION

Climbing alone all day long
In the blazing waste of spring snow,
I came down with the sunset's edge
To the highest meadow, green
In the cold mist of waterfalls,
To a cobweb of water
Woven with innumerable
Bright flowers of wild iris;
And saw far down our fire's smoke
Rising between the canyon walls,
A human thing in the empty mountains.
And as I stood on the stones
In the midst of whirling water,
The whirling iris perfume
Caught me in a vision of you
More real than reality:
Fire in the deep curves of your hair:
Your hips whirled in a tango,
Out and back in dim scented light;
Your cheeks snow-flushed, the zithers
Ringing, all the crowded ski lodge
Dancing and singing; your arms
White in the brown autumn water,
Swimming through the fallen leaves,
Making a fluctuant cobweb
Of light on the sycamores;
Your thigh's exact curve, the fine gauze
Slipping through my hands, and you
Tense on the verge of abandon;

Your breasts' very touch and smell;
The sweet secret odor of sex.
Forever the thought of you,
And the splendor of the iris,
The crinkled iris petal,
The gold hairs powdered with pollen,
And the obscure cantata
Of the tangled water, and the
Burning, impassive snow peaks,
Are knotted together here.
This moment of fact and vision
Seizes immortality,
Becomes the person of this place.
The responsibility
Of love realized and beauty
Seen burns in a burning angel
Real beyond flower or stone.

LUTE MUSIC

The earth will be going on a long time
Before it finally freezes;
Men will be on it; they will take names,
Give their deeds reasons.
We will be here only
As chemical constituents –
A small franchise indeed.
Right now we have lives,
Corpuscles, ambitions, caresses,
Like everybody had once –
All the bright *neige d'antan* people,
"Blithe Helen, white Iope, and the rest,"
All the uneasy, remembered dead.

Here at the year's end, at the feast
Of birth, let us bring to each other
The gifts brought once west through deserts –
The precious metal of our mingled hair,
The frankincense of enraptured arms and legs,
The myrrh of desperate, invincible kisses –
Let us celebrate the daily
Recurrent nativity of love,
The endless epiphany of our fluent selves,
While the earth rolls away under us
Into unknown snows and summers,
Into untraveled spaces of the stars.

FLOATING

Our canoe idles in the idling current
Of the tree and vine and rush enclosed
Backwater of a torpid midwestern stream;
Revolves slowly, and lodges in the glutted
Waterlilies. We are tired of paddling.
All afternoon we have climbed the weak current,
Up dim meanders, through woods and pastures,
Past muddy fords where the strong smell of cattle
Lay thick across the water; singing the songs
Of perfect, habitual motion; ski songs,
Nightherding songs, songs of the capstan walk,
The levee, and the roll of the voyageurs.
Tired of motion, of the rhythms of motion,
Tired of the sweet play of our interwoven strength,
We lie in each other's arms and let the palps
Of waterlily leaf and petal hold back
All motion in the heat thickened, drowsing air.
Sing to me softly, Westron Wynde, Ah the Syghes,
Mon coeur se recommend à vous, Phoebi Claro;
Sing the wandering erotic melodies
Of men and women gone seven hundred years,
Softly, your mouth close to my cheek.
Let our thighs lie entangled on the cushions,
Let your breasts in their thin cover
Hang pendant against my naked arms and throat;
Let your odorous hair fall across our eyes;
Kiss me with those subtle, melodic lips.
As I undress you, your pupils are black, wet,
Immense, and your skin ivory and humid.

Move softly, move hardly at all, part your thighs,
Take me slowly while our gnawing lips
Fumble against the humming blood in our throats.
Move softly, do not move at all, but hold me,
Deep, still, deep within you, while time slides away,
As this river slides beyond this lily bed,
And the thieving moments fuse and disappear
In our mortal, timeless flesh.

ANDRÉE REXROTH

Purple and green, blue and white,
The Oregon river mouths
Slide into thick smoky darkness
As the turning cup of day
Slips from the whirling hemisphere.
And all that white long beach gleams
In white twilight as the lights
Come on in the lonely hamlets;
And voices of men emerge;
And dogs barking, as the wind stills.
Those August evenings are
Sixteen years old tonight and I
Am sixteen years older too –
Lonely, caught in the midst of life,
In the chaos of the world;
And all the years that we were young
Are gone, and every atom
Of your learned and disordered
Flesh is utterly consumed.

LYELL'S HYPOTHESIS AGAIN

An Attempt to Explain the Former
Changes of the Earth's Surface by
Causes Now in Operation

SUBTITLE OF LYELL: *Principles of Geology*

The mountain road ends here,
Broken away in the chasm where
The bridge washed out years ago.
The first scarlet larkspur glitters
In the first patch of April
Morning sunlight. The engorged creek
Roars and rustles like a military
Ball. Here by the waterfall,
Insuperable life, flushed
With the equinox, sentient
And sentimental, falls away
To the sea and death. The tissue
Of sympathy and agony
That binds the flesh in its Nessus' shirt;
The clotted cobweb of unself
And self; sheds itself and flecks
The sun's bed with darts of blossom
Like flagellant blood above
The water bursting in the vibrant
Air. This ego, bound by personal
Tragedy and the vast
Impersonal vindictiveness
Of the ruined and ruining world,

Pauses in this immortality,
As passionate, as apathetic,
As the lava flow that burned here once;
And stopped here; and said, "This far
And no further." And spoke thereafter
In the simple diction of stone.

*

Naked in the warm April air,
We lie under the redwoods,
In the sunny lee of a cliff.
As you kneel above me I see
Tiny red marks on your flanks
Like bites, where the redwood cones
Have pressed into your flesh.
You can find just the same marks
In the lignite in the cliff
Over our heads. *Sequoia
Langsdorfii* before the ice,
And *sempervirens* afterwards,
There is little difference,
Except for all those years.

Here in the sweet, moribund
Fetor of spring flowers, washed,
Flotsam and jetsam together,
Cool and naked together,
Under this tree for a moment,
We have escaped the bitterness
Of love, and love lost, and love
Betrayed. And what might have been,

And what might be, fall equally
Away with what is, and leave
Only these ideograms
Printed on the immortal
Hydrocarbons of flesh and stone.

YUGAO

Tonight is clearer and colder.
The new half-moon slides through clouds.
The air is full of the poignant
Odor of frost drying earth.
Late night, the stillness grows more still.
At last, nothing moves, no sound,
Even the shunting freight trains
In the distance stop.
                              I go out
Into the ominous dark,
Into the garden crowded with
Invisible, impalpable
Movement. The air is breathless
Under the trees. High overhead,
The wind plunges with the moon
Through breaking and driving clouds.
I seem to stand in the midst
Of an incomprehensible
Tragedy; as though a world
Doubled against this were tearing
Through the thin shell of night;
As though something earthbound with its
Own glamorous violence
Struggled beside me in the dark.
On such nights as this the young
Warriors of old time take form
In the Noh plays; and, it may be,
Some distraught, imagined girl,
Amalfi's duchess, Electra,

Struggles like an ice bound swan,
Out of the imagination,
Toward a body, beside me,
Beyond the corner of the eye;
Or, may be, some old jealousy
Or hate I have forgotten
Still seeks flesh to walk in life.
If so, I cannot see her.
I can call, plain to the mind's eye,
Your bright sleeping head, nested
In its pillow, and your face, sure
And peaceful as your moving
Breath. You, wandering in your dream,
Watched over by your love for me.

ANDRÉE REXROTH

Mt. Tamalpais

The years have gone. It is spring
Again. Mars and Saturn will
Soon come on, low in the West,
In the dusk. Now the evening
Sunlight makes hazy girders
Over Steep Ravine above
The waterfalls. The winter
Birds from Oregon, robins
And varied thrushes, feast on
Ripe toyon and madrone
Berries. The robins sing as
The dense light falls.

               Your ashes
Were scattered in this place. Here
I wrote you a farewell poem,
And long ago another,
A poem of peace and love,
Of the lassitude of a long
Spring evening in youth. Now
It is almost ten years since
You came here to stay. Once more,
The pussy willows that come
After the New Year in this
Outlandish land are blooming.
There are deer and raccoon tracks
In the same places. A few
New sand bars and cobble beds

Have been left where erosion
Has gnawed deep into the hills.
The rounds of life are narrow.
War and peace have passed like ghosts.
The human race sinks towards
Oblivion. A bittern
Calls from the same rushes where
You heard one on our first year
In the West; and where I heard
One again in the year
Of your death.

Kings River Canyon

My sorrow is so wide
I cannot see across it;
And so deep I shall never
Reach the bottom of it.
The moon sinks through deep haze,
As though the Kings River Canyon
Were filled with fine, warm, damp gauze.
Saturn gleams through the thick light
Like a gold, wet eye; nearby,
Antares glows faintly,
Without sparkle. Far overhead,
Stone shines darkly in the moonlight –
Lookout Point, where we lay
In another full moon, and first
Peered down into this canyon.
Here we camped, by still autumnal
Pools, all one warm October.
I baked you a bannock birthday cake.

Here you did your best paintings –
Innocent, wondering landscapes.
Very few of them are left
Anywhere. You destroyed them
In the terrible trouble
Of your long sickness. Eighteen years
Have passed since that autumn.
There was no trail here then.
Only a few people knew
How to enter this canyon.
We were all alone, twenty
Miles from anybody;
A young husband and wife,
Closed in and wrapped about
In the quiet autumn,
In the sound of quiet water,
In the turning and falling leaves,
In the wavering of innumerable
Bats from the caves, dipping
Over the odorous pools
Where the great trout drowsed in the evenings.

Eighteen years have been ground
To pieces in the wheels of life.
You are dead. With a thousand
Convicts they have blown a highway
Through Horseshoe Bend. Youth is gone,
That only came once. My hair
Is turning grey and my body
Heavier. I too move on to death.
I think of Henry King's stilted
But desolated *Exequy,*

Of Yuan Chen's great poem,
Unbearably pitiful;
Alone by the spring river
More alone than I had ever
Imagined I would ever be,
I think of Frieda Lawrence,
Sitting alone in New Mexico,
In the long drought, listening
For the hiss of the milky Isar,
Over the cobbles, in a lost spring.

for Mildred

The sky is perfectly clear.
Motionless in the moonlight,
The redwood forest descends
Three thousand feet to the sea,
To the unmoving, silent,
Thick, white fog bank that stretches
Westward to the horizon.
No sound rises from the sea;
And the forest is soundless.
Here in the open windows,
Watching the night together,
I cannot understand what
You murmur, singing sweetly,
Softly, to yourself, in French.
O, lady, you are learned,
In your hands as they touch me,
In lips that sing obscurely,
In secret, your private songs.
Your face looks white and frozen
In the moonlight, and your eyes
Glitter, rigid and immense.
The illusion of moonlight
Makes you look terror stricken.
And behind you the firelight
Draws black and red frightening
Toppling patterns on the walls.
An airplane crosses, low down,

And fills the landscape with noise
Like an hallucination.
Alive or dead, the stiff heart,
As the hours slide through moonlight,
Squeezes blood and memory.
The fog climbs up the mountain,
And leaves only one star in
The fogbound wood, like an eye
In a tomb. Without warning
Your voice breaks, and your face
Streams with tears, and you stagger
Against me. I do not speak,
But hold you still in my arms.
Finally you say, "I am not
Weeping for our own troubles,
But for the general chaos
Of the world." I feel you hurling
Away, abandoned on
A parachute of ruin.
A violent shuddering
Overcomes me, as though all
The women like you who had
Ever lived, had stepped across my grave.

FOR THE CHINESE ACTRESS, GARDENIA CHANG

When Tu Fu was a small boy
He saw Kung Sung as she danced
With two swords, and years later
He remembered, and she lived
In his memory, always
Refining his perception,
As meditation on her
Sure grace had once taught Chang Hsu
The secret of powerful
And subtle calligraphy.
Now, days later, you are still
Clear and intact in my mind,
Your arch, small, transcendent face,
Your voice, so pure, light, and dry,
All your body's movement like
Thought in some more noble brain,
All your presence vivid as
The swords that whirled about you.
I know I shall remember
You for many, many years.
Your vision in my memory
Will teach and guide my vision,
Like the contemplation of
The deep heart of a jewel.

ROSA MUNDI

Bright petals of evening
Shatter, fall, drift over Florence,
And flush your cheeks a redder
Rose and gleam like fiery flakes
In your eyes. All over Florence
The swallows whirl between the
Tall roofs, under the bridge arches,
Spiral in the zenith like larks,
Sweep low in crying clouds above
The brown river and the white
Riverbed. Your moist, quivering
Lips are like the wet scarlet wings
Of a reborn butterfly who
Trembles on the rose petal as
Life floods his strange body.
Turn to me. Part your lips. My dear,
Some day we will be dead.

I feel like Pascal often felt.

About the mid houre of the nicht

FIRE

The air is dizzy with swallows.

Sunset comes on the golden
Towers, on the Signoría.
In the Badía, the light goes

From the face of Filippino's
Weary lady, exhausted with
The devotion of her worshipper.
Across the face of the Duomo
The Campanile's blue shadow
Marks the mathematics of beauty.
In San Miniato the gold
Mosaics still glitter through
The smoky gloom. At the end
Of the Way of the Cross, the dense
Cypress wood, full of lovers,
Shivering with impatience.
As the dark thickens, two by two
They take each other. Nightfall, all
The wood is filled with soft moaning,
As though it were filled with doves.

GOLDEN SECTION

Paestum of the twice-blooming
Roses, the sea god's honey-
Colored stone still strong against
The folly of the long decline
Of man. The snail climbs the Doric
Line, and the empty snail shell
Lies by the wild cyclamen.
The sandstone of the Roman
Road is marked with sun wrinkles
Of prehistoric beaches,
But no time at all has touched
The deep constant melodies
Of space as the columns swing
To the moving eye. The sea
Breathes like a drowsy woman.
The sun moves like a drowsy hand.
Poseidon's pillars have endured
All tempers of the sea and sun.
This is the order of the spheres,
The curve of the unwinding fern,
And the purple shell in the sea;
These are the spaces of the notes
Of every kind of music.
The world is made of number
And moved in order by love.
Mankind has risen to this point
And can only fall away,
As we can only turn homeward

Up Italy, through France, to life
Always pivoted on this place.

Finally the few tourists go,
The German photographers, the
Bevy of seminarians,
And we are left alone. We eat
In the pronaos towards the sea.
Greek food, small white loaves, smoked cheese,
Pickled squid, black figs, and honey
And olive oil, the common food
Of Naples, still, for those who eat.
An ancient dog, Odysseus' dog,
Spawned before there were breeds of dogs,
Appears, begs, eats, and disappears –
The exoteric proxy of
The god. And we too grow drowsy with
White wine, tarry from the wineskin.
The blue and gold shafts interweave
Across our nodding eyes. The sea
Prepares to take the sun. We go
Into the naos, open to the
Sky and make love, where the sea god
And the sea goddess, wet with sperm,
Coupled in the incense filled dark,
As the singing rose and was still.

Mist comes with the sunset. (The Yanks
Killed the mosquitoes.) Long lines of
Umber buffalo, their backs a
Rippling congruence, as in the
Paintings of Krishna, file across

The brilliant green sea meadows,
Under banners of white mist.
The fires of the bivouacs of
Spartacus twinkle in the hills.
Our train comes with the first stars.
Venus over the wine-dark sea.

All the way back the train fills
And fills up, and fills again,
With girls from the fish canneries,
And girls from the lace factories,
And girls from the fields, who have been
Working twelve hours for nothing,
Or at the best a few pennies.
They laugh and sing, all the way
Back to Naples, like broad-bottomed,
Deep-bosomed angels, wet with sweat.

I come back to the cottage in
Santa Monica Canyon where
Andrée and I were poor and
Happy together. Sometimes we
Were hungry and stole vegetables
From the neighbors' gardens.
Sometimes we went out and gathered
Cigarette butts by flashlight.
But we went swimming every day,
All year round. We had a dog
Called Proclus, a vast yellow
Mongrel, and a white cat named
Cyprian. We had our first
Joint art show, and they began
To publish my poems in Paris.
We worked under the low umbrella
Of the acacia in the dooryard.
Now I get out of the car
And stand before the house in the dusk.
The acacia blossoms powder the walk
With little pills of gold wool.
The odor is drowsy and thick
In the early evening.
The tree has grown twice as high
As the roof. Inside, an old man
And woman sit in the lamplight.
I go back and drive away
To Malibu Beach and sit

With a grey-haired childhood friend and
Watch the full moon rise over the
Long rollers wrinkling the dark bay.

THE REFLECTING TREES OF BEING
AND NOT BEING

In my childhood when I first
Saw myself unfolded in
The triple mirrors, in my
Youth, when I pursued myself
Wandering on wandering
Nightbound roads like a roving
Masterless dog, when I met
Myself on sharp peaks of ice,
And tasted myself dissolved
In the lulling heavy sea,
In the talking night, in the
Spiraling stars, what did I
Know? What do I know now,
Of myself, of the others?
Blood flows out of the fleeing
Nebulae, and flows back, red
With all the worn space of space,
Old with all the time of time.
It is my blood. I cannot
Taste in it as it leaves me
More of myself than on its
Return. I can see in it
Trees of silence and fire.
In the mirrors on its waves
I can see faces. Mostly
They are your face. On its streams
I can see the soft moonlight
On the Canal du Midi.

I can see the leaf shadows
Of the plane trees on the deep
Fluids of your eyes, and the
Golden fires and lamps of years.

II

TRANSLATIONS

HOMECOMING OF LOVE ON THE
SUMMITS OF THE WIND

Here you are, my love, preceded by the wind
Which gushes over the blond plains where bread suddenly
Blossomed in the warm hours
Of our first summer,
Climbing high into the light amongst the stones.

You rock in the narrow cradle of the ruins
Of parallel arches which Roman hands
Stretched around these temples and towers
Of their town, hoping someday maybe
You would crown them with your delicate steps
Of burning whiteness.

You take to yourself, in the midst of the murmuring stones,
And the sonorous bones locked away in their hollows,
The face of light rising up over the bald mountains,
The villages of faded bricks.
The burning paths, the vast drowsiness
Of a landscape astonished at the sight of you –
Rising like an apparition on the summit of the wind.

O my love, if I could only see you once more
Unawares, as in the old days,
Under that high sun which gave the hours
Of our first summer their harmony.

All that bright, luminous music which you were,
Rocking there in the cradle of ancient stones.

     – Rafael Alberti
      translated from the Spanish

TWO POEMS FROM
Poems from the Greek Anthology

Didyme waved her wand at me.
I am utterly enchanted.
The sight of her beauty makes me
Melt like wax before the fire. What
Is the difference if she is black?
So is coal, but alight, it shines like roses.

   – Asklepiades

It is sweet in summer to slake
Your thirst with snow, and the spring breeze
Is sweet to the sailors after
The stormy winter, but sweetest
Of all when one blanket hides two
Lovers at the worship of Kypris.

   – Asklepiades

Canzone 1

I have come at last to the short
Day and the long shadow when the
Hills turn white and the grass fades. Still
Longing stays green, stuck in this hard
Stone that speaks and hears as if it was
A woman. So it was this strange
Woman stood cold as shadowed snow,
Unmoved as stone by the sweet times
When the hills turn warm and turn from
White to green and are covered with
Flowers and grass. She, when she goes
Wreathed in herbs, drives every other
Woman from my mind – shimmering
Gold with green – so lovely that love
Comes to rest in her shadow, she
Who has caught me fast between
Two hills, faster far than fused stone.
No magic gem has her power.
No herb can heal her blow. I have
Fled through the fields, over the hills,
Trying to escape from such a
Woman, but there is no wall, no
Hill, no green leaf, can ever shade
Me from her light. Time was, I saw
Her dressed all in green, so lovely
She would have made a stone love her
As I do, who love her very

Shadow. Time was, we loved once in
The grass, she loving as ever
A woman was, and the high hills
Around us. But for sure rivers
Will flow back to the hills before
This wood, full of sap and green,
Ever catch fire again from me
As lovely women do – I who
Would be glad to sleep away my
Life turned to stone, or live on grass,
If only I could be where her
Skirts would cast their shadow on me.
Now when the shadow of the hills
Is blackest, under beautiful
Green, this young woman makes it
Vanish away at last, as if
She hid a stone in the grass.

> – *Dante*
> *translated from the Italian*

MY LOVER WILL SOON BE HERE

My lover will soon be here.
He said he would come to the garden gate.
My mother is still up.
I can hear my heart beat
Like a sword on a shield.

   – *Anonymous (Six Dynasties)*
     translated from the Chinese

THE MORNING SUN SHINES

The morning sun shines
Through the filigree shutters.
A wind full of light
Blows open her thin gauze robe.
A sly smile comes on her lips.
Her moth eyebrows arch
Over her beautiful eyes.

  – *The Emperor Wu of Liang*
   translated from the Chinese

WHEN WILL I BE HOME?

When will I be home? I don't know.
In the mountains, in the rainy night,
The autumn lake is flooded.
Someday we will be back together again.
We will sit in the candlelight by the west window,
And I will tell you how I remembered you
Tonight on the stormy mountain.

> – *Li Shang Yin*
>   *translated from the Chinese*

You know I have a husband.
Why did you give me these two glowing pearls?
I could acknowledge your love
And sew them on my red dress,
But I come from a noble family,
Courtiers of the Emperor.
My husband is an officer in the Palace Guard.
Of course I realize that your intentions
Are pure as the light of Heaven,
But I have sworn to be true to my husband
In life and in death.
So I must give back your beautiful pearls,
With two tears to match them.
Why didn't I meet you
Before I was married?

      – Chang Chi
        translated from the Chinese

TO THE TUNE "THE BOAT OF STARS"

Year after year I have watched
My jade mirror. Now my rouge
And creams sicken me. One more
Year that he has not come back.
My flesh shakes when a letter
Comes from South of the River.
I cannot drink wine since he left,
But the Autumn has drunk up all my tears.
I have lost my mind, far off
In the jungle mists of the South.
The gates of heaven are nearer
Than the body of my beloved.

– *Li Ch'ing Chao*
translated from the Chinese

CREAMY BREASTS

Fragrant with powder, moist with perspiration,
They are the pegs of a jade inlaid harp.
Aroused by spring, they are soft as cream
Under the fertilizing mist.
After my bath my perfumed lover
Holds them and plays with them
And they are cool as peonies and purple grapes.

– Chao Luan-luan (Eighth Century?)
translated from the Chinese

MARRIED LOVE

You and I
Have so much love,
That it
Burns like a fire,
In which we bake a lump of clay
Molded into a figure of you
And a figure of me.
Then we take both of them,
And break them into pieces,
And mix the pieces with water,
And mold again a figure of you,
And a figure of me.
I am in your clay.
You are in my clay.
In life we share a single quilt.
In death we will share one coffin.

      – Kuan Tao-sheng (1262–1319)
       translated from the Chinese

You held my lotus blossom
In your lips and played with the
Pistil. We took one piece of
Magic rhinoceros horn
And could not sleep all night long.
All night the cock's gorgeous crest
Stood erect. All night the bee
Clung trembling to the flower
Stamens. Oh my sweet perfumed
Jewel! I will allow only
My lord to possess my sacred
Lotus pond, and every night
You can make blossom in me
Flowers of fire.

     – Huang O (1498–1569)
      translated from the Chinese

TO THE TUNE "THE JOY OF PEACE AND BRIGHTNESS"

Bitter rain in my courtyard
In the decline of Autumn,
I have only vague poetic feelings
That I cannot bring together.
They diffuse into the dark clouds
And the red leaves.
After the yellow sunset
The cold moon rises
Out of the gloomy mist.
I will not let down the blinds
Of spotted bamboo from their silver hook.
Tonight my dreams will follow the wind,
Suffering the cold,
To the jasper tower of your beautiful flesh.

> – *Wu Tsao (Nineteenth Century)*
> *translated from the Chinese*

FROM THE PERSIAN (1)

Naked out of the dark we came.
Naked into the dark we go.
Come to my arms, naked in the dark.

   – *Anonymous*

FROM THE PERSIAN (2)

You are like the moon except
For your dark hair. You are like
Venus, except for your lips,
Crimson and perfumed, and like
The sun except that you are
Most splendid naked, at night.

   – *Anonymous*

FROM THE LATIN

I did not want you, Candida.
I did not ask you to come.
You eat your heart? My heart
Eats me. I did not want you,
Candida. You came anyway.

   – Anonymous

The first time I saw you
Was last year in May,
In May, bathing in a pool
Crowded with iris.

    – Anonymous
      translated from the Japanese

When I look at her
Asleep in the dawn,
The body of my girl
Is like a lily in
The field of May.

    – Anonymous
      translated from the Japanese

The cicada cries out,
Burning with love.
The firefly burns
With silent love.

> – *Anonymous*
>   *translated from the Japanese*

When I went with you to your ship
To say good-bye,
My tears choked me
And I said nothing.

> – *Anonymous*
>   *translated from the Japanese*

The sound of my laughter
Awoke me from the dream
Where we lay together,
And I looked around me,
My eyes filled with tears.

– *Anonymous*
  translated from the Japanese

The nightingale on the flowering plum,
The stag beneath the autumn maple,
And you and me together in bed,
Happy as two fish in the water.

– *Anonymous*
  translated from the Japanese

I will remember forever
How I met you all alone,
Your dead white face
Gleaming like foxfire
In the rainy midnight.

    – Anonymous
       translated from the Japanese

Out of doors, I think,
At home I think,
How she looked that day
As she went by
Trailing the skirts of
Her crimson dress.

    – Anonymous
       translated from the Japanese

When I gathered flowers
For my girl
From the top of the plum tree,
The lower branches
Drenched me with dew.

    – Kakinomoto no Hitomaro
      translated from the Japanese

In the spring garden,
In the colored shadow
Of peach blossoms,
A girl stands
On a white path.

    – Otomo no Yakamochi
      translated from the Japanese

I am so lost
In the black depths
Of the nights of love
That I can no longer tell
Dream from reality.

    – Ariwara no Narihira
        translated from the Japanese

In the passing Summer
I send you chrysanthemums
And asters for your birthday,
A flower bridge between us,
As we stand equidistant
Across life's solstice.

    – Anonymous
        translated from the Japanese

Once, far over the breakers,
I caught a glimpse
Of a white bird
And fell in love
With this dream which obsesses me.

> – *Yosano Akiko*
> *translated from the Japanese*

Over the old honeymoon cottage
At the mountain temple
The wild cherry blossoms are falling.
Here, in the desolate false dawn,
The stars go out in heaven.

> – *Yosano Akiko*
> *translated from the Japanese*

THE RED KITE

My dear, what have you done
With our old red kite?
Let's fly it again this evening
As high as we can,
Through the driving sleet
Towards the moon in the sky.

The shore is far away now
Where we were young together once.
The red kite is torn and battered,
But maybe it will still fly.

My dear, come, let's fly it wildly,
As far out as we can
With all the cords of the heart
Through the falling sleet
Towards the moon in the sky.

    – *Saijo Yaso*
        translated from the Japanese

EQUATION

Only truth can explain your eyes
That sow stars in the vault of heaven,
Where the clouds float through a field of tones

(The flowers which are born out of nothing,
When your eyes make fate so simple,
And the stars fly away from the hive
In the blue-green waiting room of heaven)

And explain your rapport with destiny.

> – *Gunnar Ekelof*
> *translated from the Swedish*

III

Who are you? Who am I? Haunted
By the dead, by the dead and the past and the
Falling inertia of unreal, dead
Men and things. Haunted by the threat
Of the impersonal, that which
Never will admit the person,
The closed world of things. Who are
You? Coming up out of the
Mineral earth, one pale leaf
Unlike any other unfolding,
And then another, strange, new,
Utterly different, nothing
I ever expected, growing
Up out of my warm heart's blood.
All new, all strange, all different.
Your own leaf pattern, your own
Flower and fruit, but fed from
One root, the root of our fused flesh.
I and thou, from the one to
The dual, from the dual
To the other, the wonderful,
Unending, unfathomable
Process of becoming each
Our selves for each other.

SURVIVAL OF THE FITTEST

I realize as I
Cast out over the lake
At thirteen thousand feet –
I don't know where you are.
It has been years since we
Married and had children
By people neither of
Us knew in the old days.
But I still catch fish with flies
Made from your blonde pubic hair.

A SINGING VOICE

Once, camping on a high bluff
Above the Fox River, when
I was about fourteen years
Old, on a full moonlit night
Crowded with whippoorwills and
Frogs, I lay awake long past
Midnight watching the moon move
Through the half drowned stars. Suddenly
I heard, far away on the warm
Air a high clear soprano,
Purer than the purest boy's
Voice, singing, "Tuck me to sleep
In my old 'Tucky home."
She was in an open car
Speeding along the winding
Dipping highway beneath me.
A few seconds later
An old touring car full of
Boys and girls rushed by under
Me, the soprano rising
Full and clear and now close by
I could hear the others singing
Softly behind her voice. Then
Rising and falling with the
Twisting road the song closed, soft
In the night. Over thirty
Years have gone by but I have
Never forgotten. Again
And again, driving on a

Lonely moonlit road, or waking
In a warm murmurous night,
I hear that voice singing that
Common song like an
Angelic memory.

ON A FLYLEAF OF *Rime – Gaspara Stampa*

bought in the Libreria Serenissima
Venice, June 14, 1949

While the light of Canaletto
And Guardi turns to the light of
Turner, and the domes of the Saluta
Begin to take on the evening,
I drink chocolate and Vecchia
Romagna, that estimable
Brandy, on the terrace of
The Café International,
And read these twisting,
Burning pages. Love was
An agony for you, too, Signora,
And came to no good end after
All the terrible price.
Enveloped in the evening
Sussura of this quiet city,
Where the loudest human sound
Is a footfall, I sit alone
With my own life. Last night I took
A gondola, out past the Giudecca,
Straight into the moonlight.
Coming back the monks
Were singing matins in San Giorgio
Maggiore. I wonder if it is possible
To be more alone than in a gondola
In Venice under the full moon
Of June. All I have for company
Are the two halves of my heart.

from MARY AND THE SEASONS

Dry Autumn

In the evening, just before
Sunset, while we were cooking
Supper, we heard dogs, high on
The west ridge, running a deer.
With unbelievable speed
They quartered down the hillside,
Crossed the gulch, climbed the east ridge
And circled back above us.
As they rushed down again, I
Ran to catch them. The barking
Stopped when they reached the creek bed.
As I came near I could hear
The last terrified bleating
Of a fawn. By the time I
Got there it was already dead.
When the dogs caught sight of me,
They scurried guiltily away.
The fawn was not torn. It had
Died of fear and exhaustion.

My dearest, although you are
Still too young to understand,
At this moment horrible
Black dogs with eyes of fire and
Long white teeth and slavering
Tongues are hunting you in the dark
Mountains to eat your tender heart.

Spring Rain

The smoke of our campfire lowers
And coagulates under
The redwoods, like low-lying
Clouds. Fine mist fills the air. Drops
Rattle down from all the leaves.
As the evening comes on
The treetops vanish in fog.
Two saw-whet owls utter their
Metallic sobbing cries high
Overhead. As it gets dark
The mist turns to rain. We are
All alone in the forest.
No one is near us for miles.
In the firelight mice scurry
Hunting crumbs. Tree toads cry like
Tiny owls. Deer snort in the
Underbrush. Their eyes are green
In the firelight like balls of
Foxfire. This morning I read
Mei Yao Chen's poems, all afternoon
We walked along the stream through
Woods and meadows full of June
Flowers. We chased frogs in the
Pools and played with newts and young
Grass snakes. I picked a wild rose
For your hair. You brought
New flowers for me to name.
Now it is night and our fire
Is a red throat open in

The profound blackness, full of
The throb and hiss of the rain.

Autumn Rain

Two days ago the sky was
Full of mares' tails. Yesterday
Wind came, bringing low cigar-
Shaped clouds. At midnight the rain
Began, the first fine, still rain
Of Autumn. Before the rain
The night was warm, the sky hazy.
We lay in the field and watched
The glowing October stars,
Vega, Deneb, Altair, high,
Hercules and the Crown setting,
The Great Nebula distinct
Through the haze. Every owl
In the world called and made love
And scolded. Once in a while
We would see one on the sky,
Cruising, on wings more silent
Than silence itself, low over
The meadow. The air thickened.
The stars grew dim and went out.
The owls stopped crying in the wood.
Then the rain came, falling so
Gently on the tent we did
Not notice until a slight
Breeze blew it in on our faces.
At dawn it was still raining.
It cleared as we cooked breakfast.

We climbed through tatters of cloud
To the east ridge and walked through
The dripping, sparkling fir forest.
In the meadow at the summit
We ate lunch in the pale sun,
Ever so slightly cooler,
And watched the same long autumn
Mares' tails and came back down the
Steep rocks through the soaking ferns.

Clear Autumn

This small flat clearing is not
Much bigger than a large room
In the steep narrow canyon.
On every side the slender
Laurel trunks shut us in close.
High on the southern sidehill
Patches of sunlight filter
Through the fir trees. But the sun
Will not come back here until
Winter is past. New-fallen
Leaves shine like light on the floor.
The air hums with low-flying
Insects, too weakened to rise.
The stream has stopped. Underground,
A trickle seeps from pool to pool.
All the summer birds have gone.
Only woodpeckers and jays
And juncos have stayed behind.
Soon the rains will start, and then
Fine, silent, varied thrushes

Will come from the dark rain forests
Of the Northwest, but not yet.
We climb to the long west ridge
That looks out on the ocean
And eat lunch at a high spring
Under the rocks at the top.
Holstein calves cluster around
And watch us impassively.
No wind moves in the dry grass.
The sky and the distant sea,
The yellow hills, stretching away,
Seem seen in a clouded mirror.
Buzzards on the rising air
Float without moving a wing.
Jet bombers play at killing
So high overhead only
Long white scrawls can be seen, the
Graffiti of genocide.
The planes are invisible.
Away from the sun the air
Glitters with millions of glass
Needles, falling from the zenith.
It is as though oxygen
And nitrogen were being
Penetrated and replaced
By some shining chemical.
It is the silk of a swarm
Of ballooning spiders, flashes
Of tinsel and drifting crystal
In the vast rising autumn air.
When we get back everything
Is linked with everything else

By fine bright strands of spun glass,
The golden floor of October,
Brilliant under a gauze of light.

Blackbirds whistle over the young
Willow leaves, pale celadon green,
In the cleft of the emerald hills.
My daughter is twenty-one months old.
Already she knows the names of
Many birds and flowers and all
The animals of barnyard and zoo.
She paddles in the stream, chasing
Tiny bright green frogs. She wants
To catch them and kiss them. Now she
Runs to me with a tuft of rose
Gray owl's clover. "What's that? Oh! What's that?"
She hoots like an owl and caresses
The flower when I tell her its name.
Overhead in the deep sky
Of May Day jet bombers cut long
White slashes of smoke. The blackbird
Sings and the baby laughs, midway
In the century of horror.

THIS NIGHT ONLY

[*Eric Satie:* GYMNOPÉDIE #1]

Moonlight   now   on Malibu
The winter night   the few stars
Far away   millions   of miles
The sea   going on   and on
Forever   around   the earth
Far   and   far   as your lips   are near
Filled   with the same light   as your eyes
Darling   darling   darling
The future   is long gone by
And the past   will never happen
We have   only this
Our one forever
So small   so infinite
So brief   so vast
Immortal   as our hands that touch
Deathless   as the firelit wine we drink
Almighty   as this single kiss
That has no beginning
That will never
Never
End

As I watch at the long window
Crowds of travelers hurry
Behind me, rainy darkness
Blows before me, and the great plane
Circles, taxis to the runway,
Waits, and then roars off into
The thick night. I follow it
As it rises through the clouds
And levels off under the stars.
Stars, darkness, a row of lights,
Moaning engines, thrumming wings,
A silver plane over a sea
Of starlit clouds and rain bound
Sea. What I am following
Is a rosy, glowing coal
Shaped like the body of a
Woman – rushing southward a
Meteor afire with the
Same fire that burns me unseen
Here on the whirling earth amongst
Bright, busy, incurious
Faces of hundreds of people
Who pass me, unaware of
The blazing astrophysics
Of the end of a weekend.

It's rained every day since you
Went away. I've been lonely.
Lonely, empty, tenderness –
Longing to kiss the corners
Of your mouth as you smile
Your special, inward, sensual,
And ironic smile I love
Because I know it means you
Are content – *content* in French –
A special, inward, sensual,
And ironic state of bliss.
Tu es contente, ma chèrie?
I am, even if lonely,
Because I can call to mind
Your body in a warm room,
In the rainy winter night,
A rose on the hearth of winter,
A rose cloud standing naked,
In the perfume of your flesh.
Moi aussi, je suis content.

COMING

You are driving to the airport
Along the glittering highway
Through the warm night,
Humming to yourself.
The yellow rose buds that stood
On the commode faded and fell
Two days ago. Last night the
Petals dropped from the tulips
On the dresser. The signs of
Your presence are leaving the
House one by one. Being without
You was almost more than I
Could bear. Now the work is squared
Away. All the arrangements
Have been made. All the delays
Are past and I am thirty
Thousand feet in the air over
A dark lustrous sea, under
A low half moon that makes the wings
Gleam like fish under water –
Rushing south four hundred miles
Down the California coast
To your curving lips and your
Ivory thighs.

This is the sea called peaceful,
And tonight it is quiet
As sleeping flesh under
The October waning moon.
Late night, not a moving car
On all the moonlit Coast Highway.
No sound but the offshore bells
And the long, recurrent hiss
Of windless surf. "Sophocles
Long ago heard it by the
Aegean." I drive eighty
Miles an hour through the still,
Moonfilled air. The surf withdraws,
Returns, and brings into my
Mind the turgid ebb and flow
Of human loyalty –
The myriad ruined voices
That have said, "Ah, love, let us
Be true to one another."
The moon-lured voyagers sleep
In all the voiceless city.
Far out on the horizon
The lights of the albacore
Fleet gleam like a golden town
In another country.

MAROON BELLS

How can I love you more than
The silver whistle of the
Coney in the rocks loves you?
How can I love you better
Than the blue of the bluebells
By the waterfall loves you?
Eater of moonlight, drinker
Of brightness, feet of jewels
On the mountain, velvet feet
In the meadow grass, darkness
Braided with wild roses, wild
Mare of all the horizons....
A far away tongue speaks in
The time that fills me like a
Tongue in a bell falling
Out of all the towers of space.
Eyes wide, nostrils distended,
We drown in secret happy
Oceans we trade in broad daylight.
O my girl, mistress of all
Illuminations and all
Commonplaces, I love you
Like the air and the water
And the earth and the fire and
The light love you and love you.

ASPEN MEADOWS

Look. Listen. They are lighting
The moon. Be still. I don't want
To hear again that wistful
Kyriale of husbands and lovers.
Stop questioning me
About my women. You are
Not a schoolgirl nor I a
Lecturing paleobotanist.
It's enough that the green glow
Runs through the down on your arms
Like a grass fire and your eyes
Are fogs of the same endless light.
Let the folds and divisions
Of your anatomy envelop
All horizons. O my sweet
Topology and delusion,
You may be arrogant and feral
But no clock can measure
How long ago you fell asleep
In my arms in the midst of
Sliding doors, parting curtains,
Electric fishes and candy lotuses
And the warm wet moonlight.

LIKE QUEEN CHRISTINA

Orange and blue and then grey
The frosty twilight comes down
Through the thin trees. The fresh snow
Holds the light longer than the sky.
Skaters on the pond vanish
In dusk, but their voices stay,
Calling and laughing, and birds
Twitter and cry in the reeds.
Indoors as night fills the white rooms,
You stand in the candlelight
Laughing like a splendid jewel.

All night rain falls through fog.
I lie awake, restless on a twisted pillow.
Foghorns cry over the desolate water.
How long ago was it,
That night with the pear blossoms
Quivering in the pulsating moonlight?
I am startled from sleep
By the acrid fleshy odor of pear blossoms.

Somewhere in the world, I suppose,
You are still living, a middle-aged matron,
With children on the verge of youth.

ANDRÉE REXROTH

died October, 1940

Now once more grey mottled buckeye branches
Explode their emerald stars,
And alders smoulder in a rosy smoke
Of innumerable buds.
I know that spring again is splendid
As ever, the hidden thrush
As sweetly tongued, the sun as vital –
But these are the forest trails we walked together,
These paths, ten years together.
We thought the years would last forever,
They are all gone now, the days
We thought would not come for us are here.
Bright trout poised in the current –
The raccoon's track at the water's edge –
A bittern booming in the distance –
Your ashes scattered on this mountain –
Moving seaward on this stream.

PRECESSION OF THE EQUINOXES

Time was, I walked in February rain,
My head full of its own rhythms like a shell,
And came home at night to write of love and death,
High philosophy, and brotherhood of man.

After intimate acquaintance with these things,
I contemplate the changes of the weather,
Flowers, birds, rabbits, mice, and other small deer
Fulfilling the year's periodicity.

And the reassurances of my own pulse.

CONFUSION

for Nancy Shores

I pass your home in a slow vermilion dawn,
The blinds are drawn, and the windows are open.
The soft breeze from the lake
Is like your breath upon my cheek.
All day long I walk in the intermittent rainfall.
I pick a vermilion tulip in the deserted park,
Bright raindrops cling to its petals.
At five o'clock it is a lonely color in the city.
I pass your home in a rainy evening,
I can see you faintly, moving between lighted walls.
Late at night I sit before a white sheet of paper,
Until a fallen vermilion petal quivers before me.

THE LIGHTS IN THE SKY ARE STARS

for Mary

Halley's Comet

When in your middle years
The great comet comes again
Remember me, a child,
Awake in the summer night,
Standing in my crib and
Watching that long-haired star
So many years ago.
Go out in the dark and see
Its plume over water
Dribbling on the liquid night,
And think that life and glory
Flickered on the rushing
Bloodstream for me once, and for
All who have gone before me,
Vessels of the billion-year-long
River that flows now in your veins.

The Great Nebula of Andromeda

We get into camp after
Dark, high on an open ridge
Looking out over five thousand
Feet of mountains and mile
Beyond mile of valley and sea.
In the star-filled dark we cook

Our macaroni and eat
By lantern light. Stars cluster
Around our table like fireflies.
After supper we go straight
To bed. The night is windy
And clear. The moon is three days
Short of full. We lie in bed
And watch the stars and the turning
Moon through our little telescope.
Late at night the horses stumble
Around camp and I awake.
I lie on my elbow watching
Your beautiful sleeping face
Like a jewel in the moonlight.
If you are lucky and the
Nations let you, you will live
Far into the twenty-first
Century. I pick up the glass
And watch the Great Nebula
Of Andromeda swim like
A phosphorescent amoeba
Slowly around the Pole. Far
Away in distant cities
Fat-hearted men are planning
To murder you while you sleep.

The Heart of Herakles

Lying under the stars,
In the summer night,
Late, while the autumn
Constellations climb the sky,

As the Cluster of Hercules
Falls down the west
I put the telescope by
And watch Deneb
Move towards the zenith.
My body is asleep. Only
My eyes and brain are awake.
The stars stand around me
Like gold eyes. I can no longer
Tell where I begin and leave off.
The faint breeze in the dark pines,
And the invisible grass,
The tipping earth, the swarming stars
Have an eye that sees itself.

A Maze of Sparks of Gold

Spring – the rain goes by, the stars
Shine pale beside the Easter
Moon. Scudding clouds, tossing leaves,
Whirl overhead. Blossoms fall
In the dark from the fragrant
Madrone trees. You lie beside
Me, luminous and still in sleep.
Overhead bees sleep in their
Tree. Beyond them the bees in
The Beehive in the Crab drift
Slowly past, a maze of points
Of fire. I've had ten times your
Years. Time holds us both fixed fast
Under the bright wasting stars.

A Sword in a Cloud of Light

Your hand in mine, we walk out
To watch the Christmas Eve crowds
On Fillmore Street, the Negro
District. The night is thick with
Frost. The people hurry, wreathed
In their smoky breaths. Before
The shop windows the children
Jump up and down with spangled
Eyes. Santa Clauses ring bells.
Cars stall and honk. Streetcars clang.
Loudspeakers on the lampposts
Sing carols, on jukeboxes
In the bars Louis Armstrong
Plays *White Christmas*. In the joints
The girls strip and grind and bump
To *Jingle Bells*. Overhead
The neon signs scribble and
Erase and scribble again
Messages of avarice,
Joy, fear, hygiene, and the proud
Names of the middle classes.
The moon beams like a pudding.
We stop at the main corner
And look up, diagonally
Across, at the rising moon,
And the solemn, orderly
Vast winter constellations.
You say, "There's Orion!"
The most beautiful object
Either of us will ever

Know in the world or in life
Stands in the moonlit empty
Heavens, over the swarming
Men, women, and children, black
And white, joyous and greedy,
Evil and good, buyer and
Seller, master and victim,
Like some immense theorem,
Which, if once solved would forever
Solve the mystery and pain
Under the bells and spangles.
There he is, the man of the
Night before Christmas, spread out
On the sky like a true god
In whom it would only be
Necessary to believe
A little. I am fifty
And you are five. It would do
No good to say this and it
May do no good to write it.
Believe in Orion. Believe
In the night, the moon, the crowded
Earth. Believe in Christmas and
Birthdays and Easter rabbits.
Believe in all those fugitive
Compounds of nature, all doomed
To waste away and go out.
Always be true to these things.
They are all there is. Never
Give up this savage religion
For the blood-drenched civilized
Abstractions of the rascals
Who live by killing you and me.

Protoplasm of Light

How long ago
Frances and I took the subway
To Van Cortlandt Park. The people
All excited, small boys and
Cripples selling dark glasses.
We rushed to the open hills
North of the station as though
We'd be too late, and stood there
Hand in hand, waiting. Under
The trees the sun made little
Lunes of light through the bare branches
On the snow. The sky turned grey
And very empty. One by
One the stars came out. At last
The sun was only a thin
Crescent in our glasses with the
Bright planets nearby like watchers.
Then the great cold amoeba
Of crystal light sprang out
On the sky. The wind passed like
A silent crowd. The crowd sobbed
Like a passing wind. All the dogs
Howled. The silent protoplasm
Of light stood still in the black sky,
In its bowels, ringed with ruby
Fire, its stone-black nucleus.
Mercury, cold and dark like a
Fleck of iron, stood silent by it.
That was long ago.
Mary and I stand on the

Seashore and watch the sun sink
In the windy ocean. Layers
Of air break up the disc. It looks
Like a vast copper pagoda.
Spume blows past our faces, jellyfish
Pulse in the standing water,
Sprawl on the wet sand at our feet.
Twilight comes and all of the
Visible planets come out.
Venus first, and then Jupiter,
Mars and Saturn and finally
Mercury once more. Seals bark
On the rocks. I tell Mary
How Kepler never saw Mercury,
How, as he lay dying it shone
In his window, too late for him
To see. The mysterious
Cone of light leans up from the
Horizon into the pale sky.
I say, "Nobody knows what
It is or even where it is.
Maybe it is the great cloud
Of gas around the sun which
You will see some day if you
Are lucky. It stands out only
During an eclipse. I saw it
Long ago."

Blood on a Dead World

A blowing night in late fall,
The moon rises with a nick
In it. All day Mary has
Been talking about the eclipse.
Every once in a while I
Go out and report on the
Progress of the earth's shadow.
When it is passing the half,
Marthe and Mary come out
And we stand on the corner
In the first wisps of chilling
Fog and watch the light go out.
Streamers of fog reach the moon,
But never quite cover it.
We have explained with an orange,
A grapefruit, and a lamp, not
That we expect a four-
Year-old child to understand –
Just as a sort of ritual
Duty. But we are surprised.
"The earth's shadow is like blood,"
She says. I tell her the Indians
Called an eclipse blood on the moon.
"Is it all the blood on the earth
Makes the shadow that color?"
She asks. I do not answer.

CONFUSION OF THE SENSES

Moonlight fills the laurels
Like music. The moonlit
Air does not move. Your white
Face moves towards my face.
Voluptuous sorrow
Holds us like a cobweb
Like a song, a perfume, the moonlight.
Your hair falls and holds our faces.
Your lips curl into mine.
Your tongue enters my mouth.
A bat flies through the moonlight.
The moonlight fills your eyes
They have neither iris nor pupil
They are only globes of cold fire
Like the deer's eyes that go by us
Through the empty forest.
Your slender body quivers
And smells of seaweed.
We lie together listening
To each other breathing in the moonlight.
Do you hear? We are breathing. We are alive.

QUIETLY

Lying here quietly beside you,
My cheek against your firm, quiet thighs,
The calm music of Boccherini
Washing over us in the quiet,
As the sun leaves the housetops and goes
Out over the Pacific, quiet –
So quiet the sun moves beyond us,
So quiet as the sun always goes,
So quiet, our bodies, worn with the
Times and the penances of love, our
Brains curled, quiet in their shells, dormant,
Our hearts slow, quiet, reliable
In their interlocked rhythms, the pulse
In your thigh caressing my cheek. Quiet.

About the Editors

SAM HAMILL's recent books include *Destination Zero: Poems* 1970–1995 (White Pine Press), new poems, *Gratitude* (BOA Editions, 1998), and essays, *A Poet's Work: The Other Side of Poetry* (Carnegie-Mellon University Press, 1998), along with translations of Yosano Akiko's selected poems, *River of Stars,* Issa's *Spring of My Life,* and *The Essential Teachings of Chuang Tzu* (with J.P. Seaton), all from Shambhala Publications. He is editor and principal translator of *The Erotic Spirit* (Shambhala), and editor of *The Selected Poems of Thomas McGrath* and *The Gift of Tongues: Twenty-five Years of Poetry from Copper Canyon Press.* He lives near Port Townsend, Washington.

ELAINE LAURA KLEINER is Professor of English at Indiana State University, and a graduate of Oregon State University and the University of Chicago. She is the author of two volumes of poetry, *This Sacred Earth* (Avon Books, London), and *Beside Great Waters* (Mellen Poetry Press), and has published a literary study, *The Fantasy Novellas of Mircea Eliade* (Greenwood Press). She has been a Fulbright Senior Scholar in American Literature in Romania (1989–90) and the recipient of a research fellowship from the National Endowment for the Humanities. She lives near the Wabash River in southwestern Indiana.

INDEX OF TITLES

Book design & composition by John D. Berry & Tricia Treacy, using Adobe PageMaker 6.0 on a Macintosh iivx and PageMaker 6.5 on a Power 120. The typeface is Minion multiple master, designed by Robert Slimbach as part of the Adobe Originals type library. Minion is based on typefaces of the later Renaissance, but is derived from no single source. Slimbach designed Minion in 1990, then expanded it in 1992 to become a multiple master font – the first to include a size axis for optical scaling. *Printed by Malloy Lithographing.*